BOOK 1

I
Am
Maathematics
NUMBERS

Jashua Sa-Ra

I Am Maathematics
Book 1
NUMBERS

By Jashua Sa-Ra

Published by
Earthiopia Works
P.O. Box 489
Brooklyn, NY 11226

www.JashuaSaRa.com

Cover by Jashua Sa-Ra

ISBN 9781711062389

I Am Maathematics is a developmental series of books designed to help students have an in depth understanding of numbers and basic math principles. It is a resource accesible for all elementary level settings that can help strenghten students' grasp of numbers and math. Children who use the entire series will be fully equipped to enter into higher mathematics with confidence and hopefully even joy!

Ma'at

Ma'at is a word we get from ancient Egypt (Kemet). It is usually translated as balance, justice, cosmic order, divine truth. It's symbol is the feather. Every person's heart is weighed on the scale of Ma'at against her feather. If their heart was light, then they would travel in peace. If their heart was heavy, then they would suffer.

To think about what it means in daily life, it's the reason we breathe in oxygen and plants breathe in carbon, but we're breathing it in from the same air! It's what keeps electrons moving and planets spinning in their places. The delicate circle of life that keeps each other existing together in a beautiful balance is Ma'at. And because nature is what informs all of our mathematics, it is easy to see how the concept of Ma'at has now become what we call mathematics, the balance (wings) is the equal sign.

How To Use This Book

Numbers are one of the oldest tools that humanity has ever used! We use them to count people and things, measure amounts, program computers, make music...and so much more. In fact, our own bodies are full of numbers; math is happening to us and through us all the time!

This book is intended to help early learners develop number sense, by learning numbers not just as the numerals we write, but also as patterns and tools that we can use as technology.

This book teaches the words for each number, 0-10 in four spoken languages: **English, Kiswahili, Spanish, and French**. It also includes some visual represenations of the numbers. You will see empty overlapping circles (the basis of *sacred geometry*), solid touching circles, and common things that we find in the world around us, to start children identifying patterns.

Binary is a counting system that only uses two numbers: 0 and 1. Like our common decimal system has place values (e.g. 1's, 10's, 100's, 1000's, etc.), binary also has place values. However the place values in binary counting increase by two, not by ten(e.g. 1's, 2's, 4's, 8's, 16's, 32's, 64's...). The place values used for this book go (from right to left like decimal) 1, 2, 4, 8. If there is a "0" in the place then nothing is counted, but all the places where there is a "1" are added together. The place values are listed in red above the number to help you out! The same method can be used to count up to 1023 in binary using your fingers. Each finger counts as a place value, starting with the right hand thumb. When a finger is up, that finger is counted, when a finger is down, it is not counted. You add all the "up" fingers, and that is your final number!

Roman numerals still show up in many places (clocks, copyright, documents), and children should be able to identify those signs also.

American Sign Language is included as well, so that children can consider that numbers are accessible to all people, in all languages, no matter if they can even speak or hear!
(Hint: use the fingernails to identify which direction the hand should be facing the receiver!)

Also, to help students connect the numerals with a visual way to consider them, an **angle reference** is included. An **angle** is the space between where two lines meet. It shows a relationship to the shape of the numeral and how many angles are created by the lines needed to write it. There is also a circle next to it, divided into that many equal parts, and showing the angle degree that it creates. (Note: 0 and 10 do not have the numeral angle reference, however 10 does have the equally divided circle.)

At the back of the book, all of the different methods are grouped together for easy reference.

Get ready for family fun with numbers!!!

English	Kiswahili	Spanish	French
Zero	Sufuri	Cero	Zéro

0

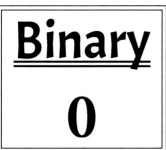

Binary
0

Roman Numerals
There is no symbol in Roman numerals for zero. They use the word "nulla" to say there is nothing.

POTENTIAL

Zero is a such a mysterious number, that sometimes it's not even called a number! Its symbol is a circle, so it doesn't have any angles to count like the other numbers. Adding it to or taking it away from another number doesn't change anything. On one hand it means "nothing" and at the same time it means "potential for everything."

Binary Fingers

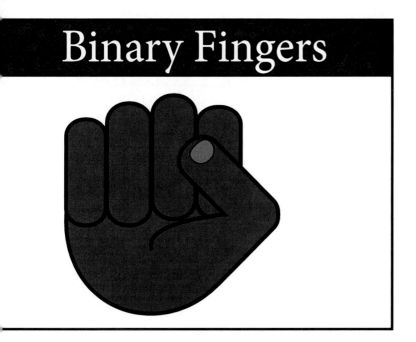

Sign Language

English	Kiswahili	Spanish	French
One	Moja	Uno	Un

1

UNITY

One is the number of unity, confidence, authority, and being unique. All of your body parts work in unity to make up one person, YOU!

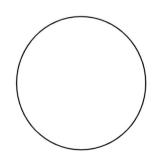

Can you name some things that there are only one of in the whole world?? What about outside of this world?!

Binary Fingers

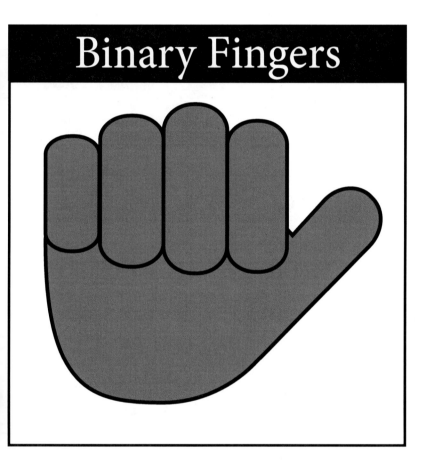

Sign Language

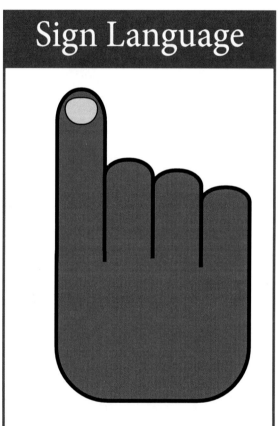

Angles

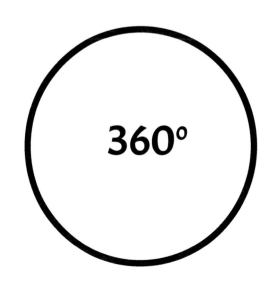

360º

English	Kiswahili	Spanish	French
Two	Mbili	Dos	Deux

COOPERATION

Two is the number of duality and cooperation. Your two hands cooperate with each other to make a clap!

Can you find things on your body that come in twos??

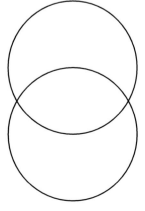

Duality is ALL over the place! Up and down, in and out, day and night, hot and cold...what else can you find?!

Binary	Roman Numerals
8 4 2 1	
0010	**II**

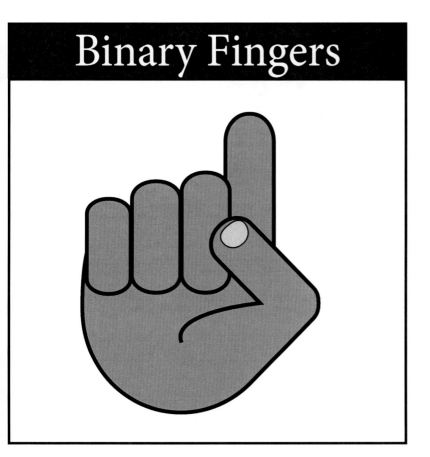

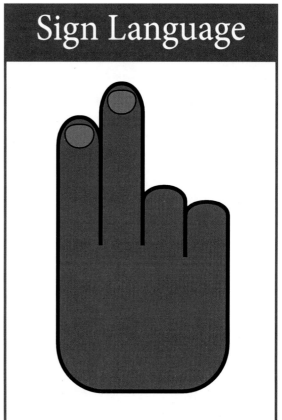

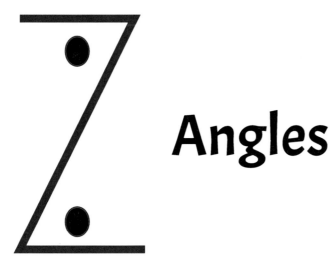

Angles

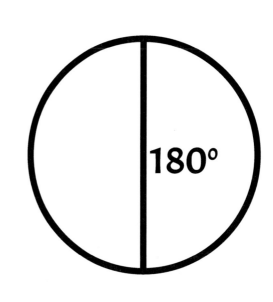

English	Kiswahili	Spanish	French
Three	Tatu	Tres	Trois

CONNECTION

Three is the number of family, relationships, and creativity. When two people have a child, they begin a family!

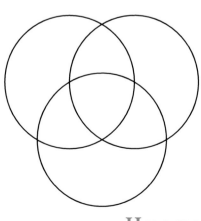

*Up, middle, down
*Left, center, right
*High, medium, low
Where do you see three things that are connected?

How many triangles do you see where you are right now?

Binary	Roman Numerals
8 4 2 1	
0011	**III**

Binary Fingers

Sign Language

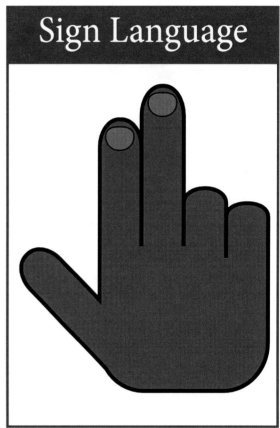

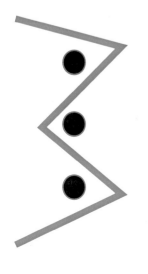

Angles

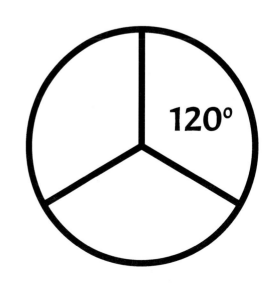

120°

English	Kiswahili	Spanish	French
Four	Nne	Quatro	Quatre

SOLID

Four is the number of being solid and stable. Your tables and chairs have four legs to keep them stable.

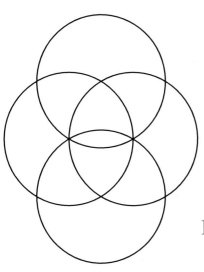

What other things in the world have four legs?

How many squares can you find around you?

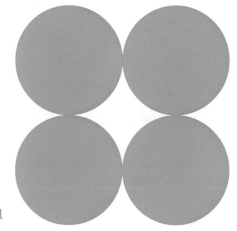

Binary 8 4 2 1 **0100**	**Roman Numerals** IV

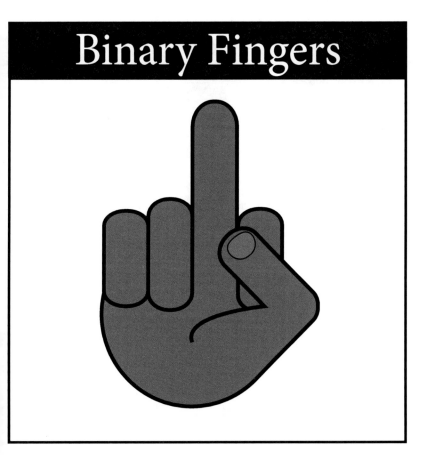

Binary Fingers

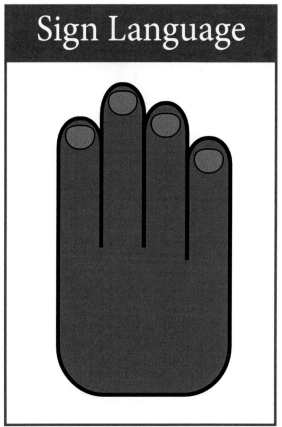

Sign Language

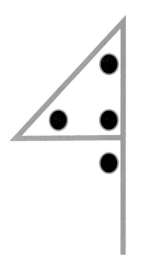

Angles

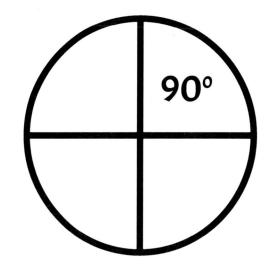

90°

English	Kiswahili	Spanish	French
Five	Tano	Cinco	Cinq

 5

GROWTH

Five is the number of change and growth. You use the five fingers of your hand to change the world around you!

Fives show up all over the place in nature! Can you name any plants that have five leaves or flower petals?

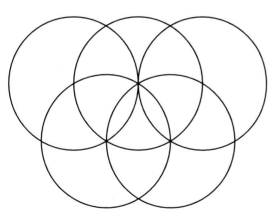

Binary	Roman Numerals
8 4 2 1 **0101**	**V**

Binary Fingers

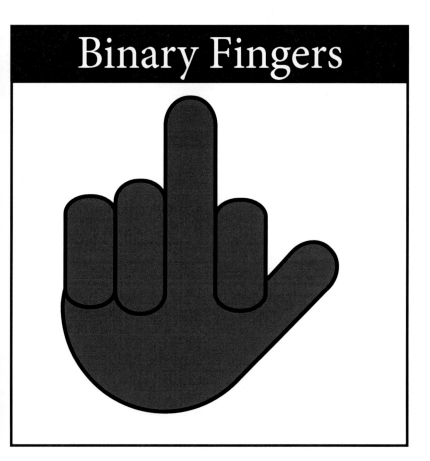

Sign Language

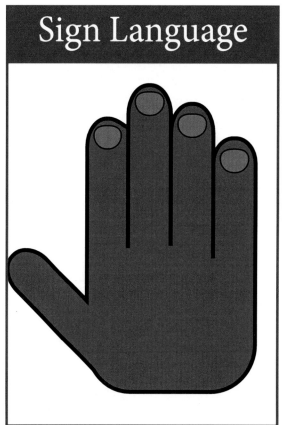

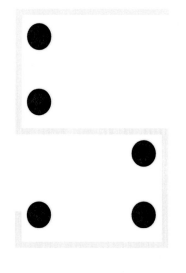

Angles

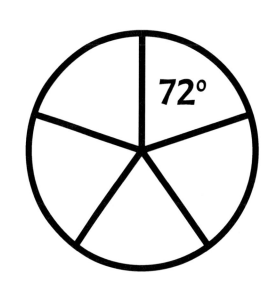

72°

English	Kiswahili	Spanish	French
Six	Sita	Seis	Six

6
HARMONY

Six is the number of harmony, love, and community. Bees work as a community to create six-sided honeycombs.

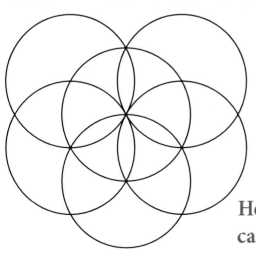

There are lots of flowers with six petals also. Try to count the petals on all the flowers you see today!

How many insects can you name that have six legs?

Binary	Roman Numerals
8 4 2 1 **0110**	**VI**

Binary Fingers

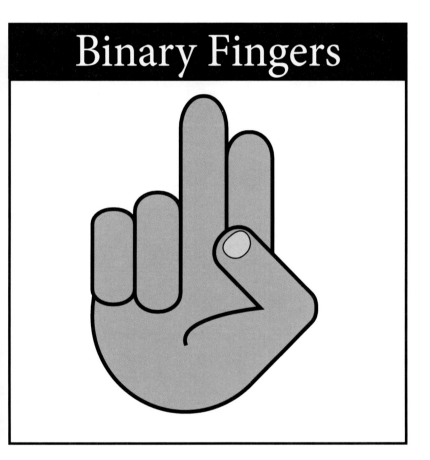

Sign Language

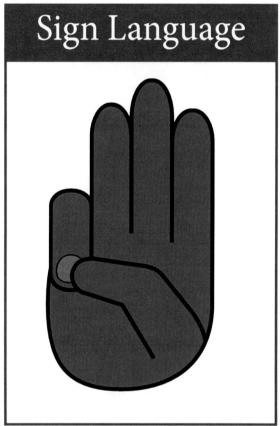

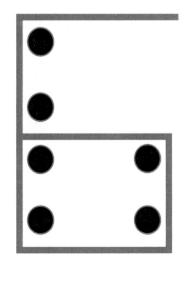

Angles

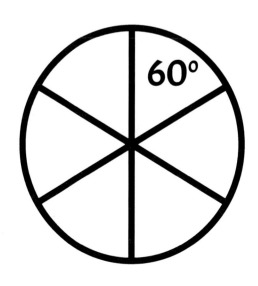

60°

English	Kiswahili	Spanish	French
Seven	Saba	Siete	Sept

7

CYCLES

Seven is the number of full cycles. The week repeats after 7 days, the rainbow always has 7 colors in it, and a piano has 7 notes before it's back at the same note.

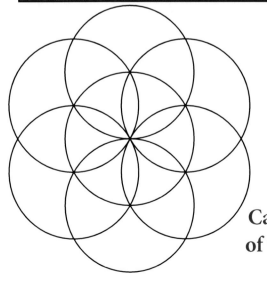

Do you know all the colors of the rainbow in order?

Can you name all the days of the week? Try it in more than one language!

Binary	Roman Numerals
8 4 2 1	
0111	**VII**

Binary Fingers

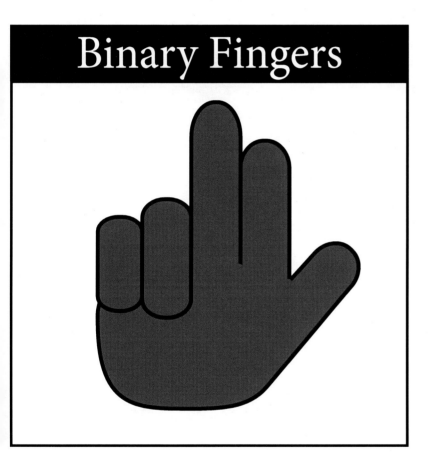

Sign Language

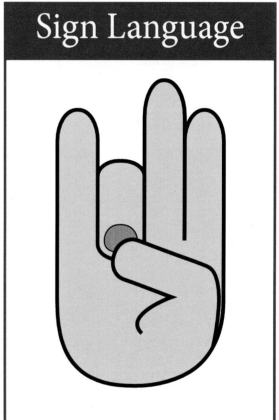

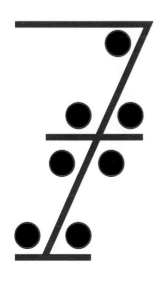

Angles

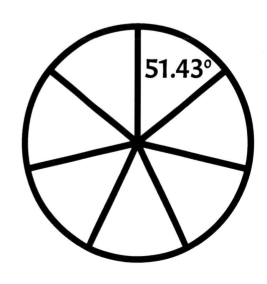

51.43°

English	Kiswahili	Spanish	French
Eight	Nane	Ocho	Huit

ABUNDANCE

Eight is the number of prosperity and abundance. An octopus has 3 hearts, 9 brains, and 8 arms, but if one arm gets cut off they can grow it back!

Do you know which street sign has eight sides?

How many animals can you name that have eight arms or legs?

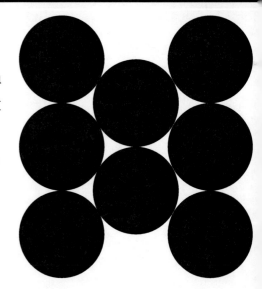

Binary	**Roman Numerals**
8 4 2 1 **1000**	**VIII**

Binary Fingers

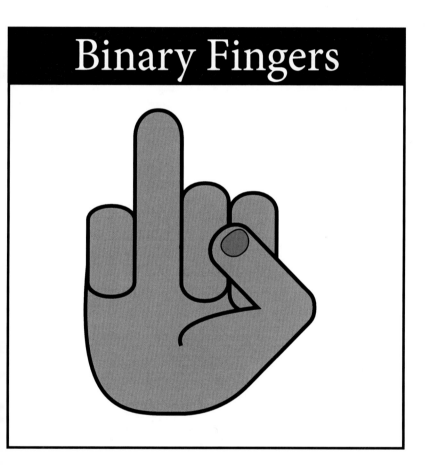

Sign Language

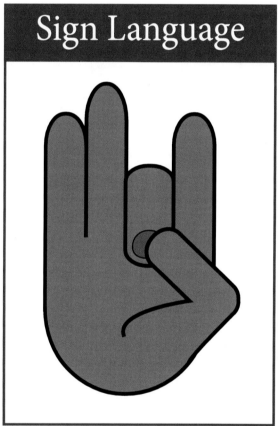

Angles

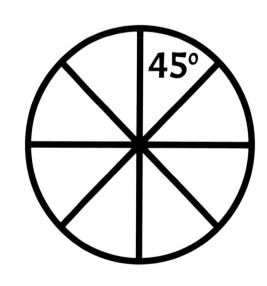

45°

English	Kiswahili	Spanish	French
Nine	Tisa	Nueve	Neuf

9

$$12345678 = 9 = 87654321$$

EVERYTHING

Nine is the last numeral, and it's a number that brings all of the other numbers together perfectly. Watch: 1+8=9, 2+7=9, 3+6=9, 4+5=9!!! What's even more magical, is that 1+2+3+4+5+6+7+8=36, and if you add those two numbers together 3+6=9!!!!!!!!

Nine likes to hide inside of other numbers! Do you think you can find some of nine's hiding places around you? You might have to be a number detective!
(Hint: match the colored numbers above!)

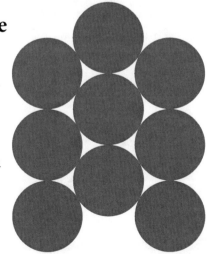

Binary	Roman Numerals
8 4 2 1 **1001**	**IX**

Binary Fingers

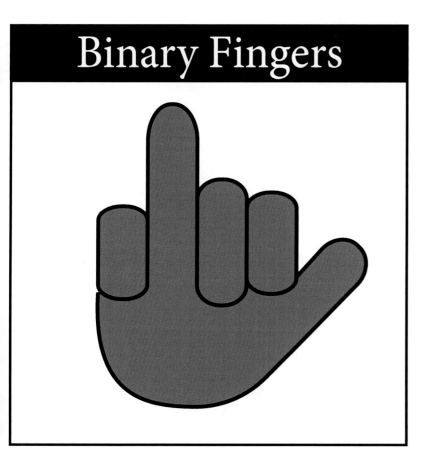

Sign Language

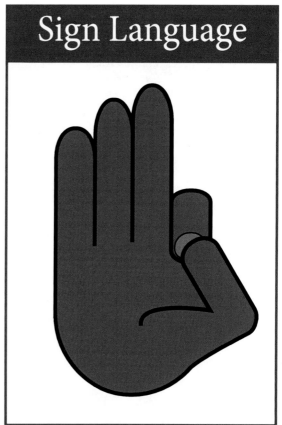

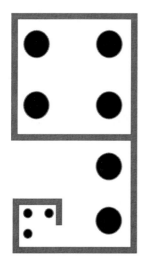

Angles

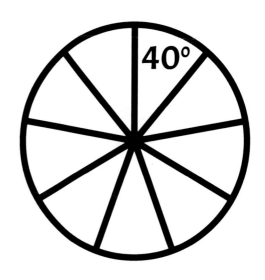

40°

English	Kiswahili	Spanish	French
Ten	Kumi	Diez	Diz

10
RENEWAL

Ten is the first number that is a combination of other numbers. It's the number of renewal and reaching a higher level. Our ten toes lead the way to new adventures every day!

Count how many times you see ten show up around you today...even fingers and toes!

Binary	Roman Numerals
8 4 2 1 **1010**	**X**

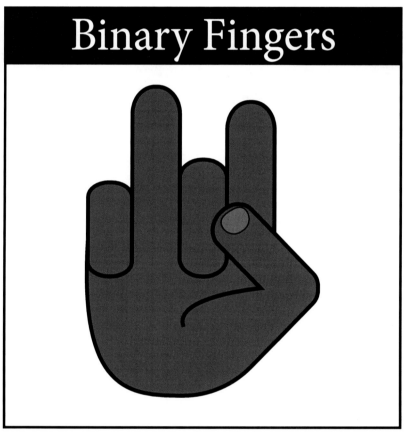

Binary Fingers

Sign Language

Keep going for yourself and see how far you can get!!! When you run out of fingers on your right hand, start on your left thumb and keep going until all ten fingers are up!

Angles

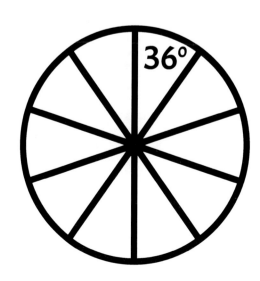

36°

Numeral	English	Swahili	Spanish	French	Binary	Roman
0	Zero	Sufuri	Cero	Zéro	0	nulla
1	One	Moja	Uno	Un	1	I
2	Two	Mbili	Dos	Deux	10	II
3	Three	Tatu	Tres	Trois	11	III
4	Four	Nne	Quatro	Quatre	100	IV
5	Five	Tano	Cinco	Cinq	101	V
6	Six	Sita	Seis	Six	110	VI
7	Seven	Saba	Siete	Sept	111	VII
8	Eight	Nane	Ocho	Huit	1000	VIII
9	Nine	Tisa	Nueve	Neuf	1001	IX
10	Ten	Kumi	Diez	Dix	1010	X

	Binary	Roman
0	0	nulla
1	1	I
2	10	II
3	11	III
4	100	IV
5	101	V
6	110	VI
7	111	VII
8	1000	VIII
9	1001	IX
10	1010	X

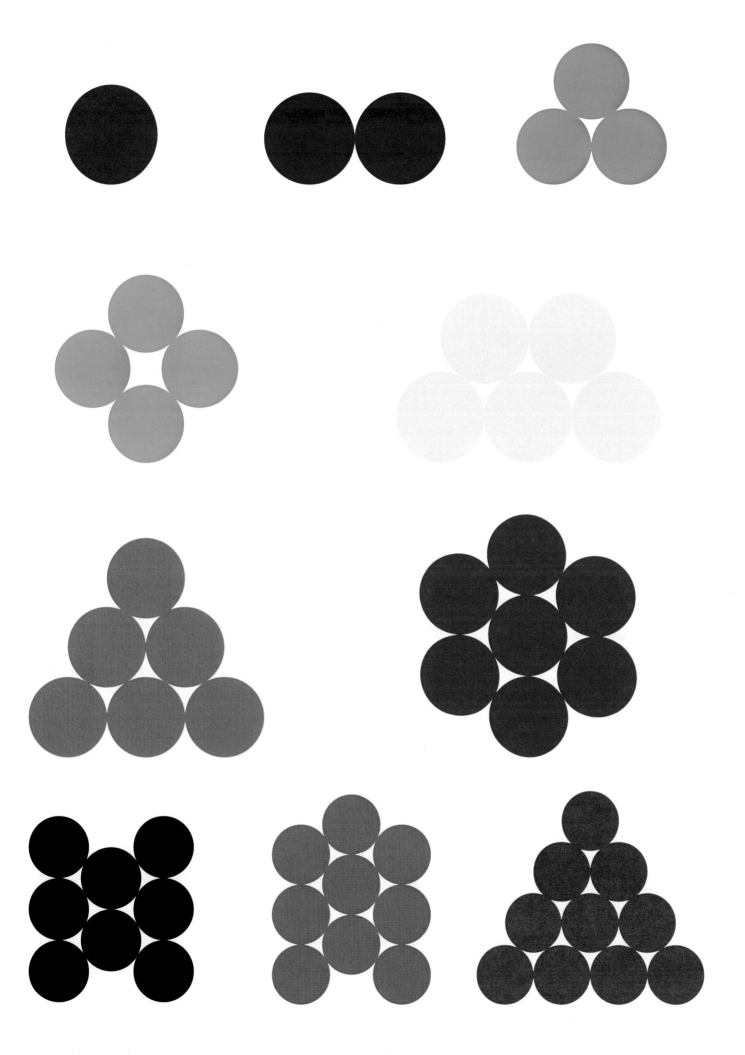

Binary Fingers

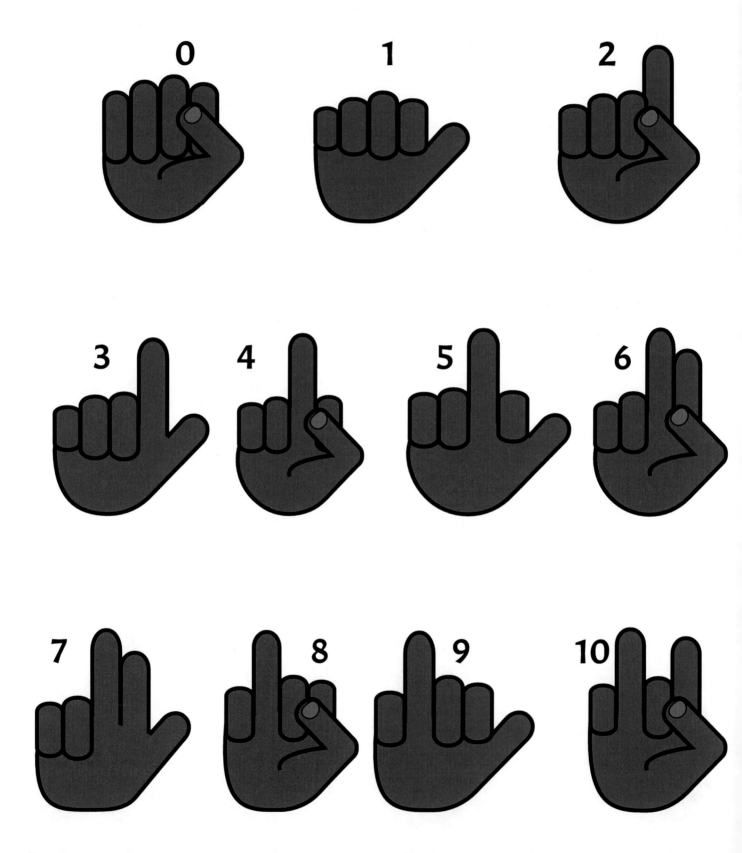

Sign Language

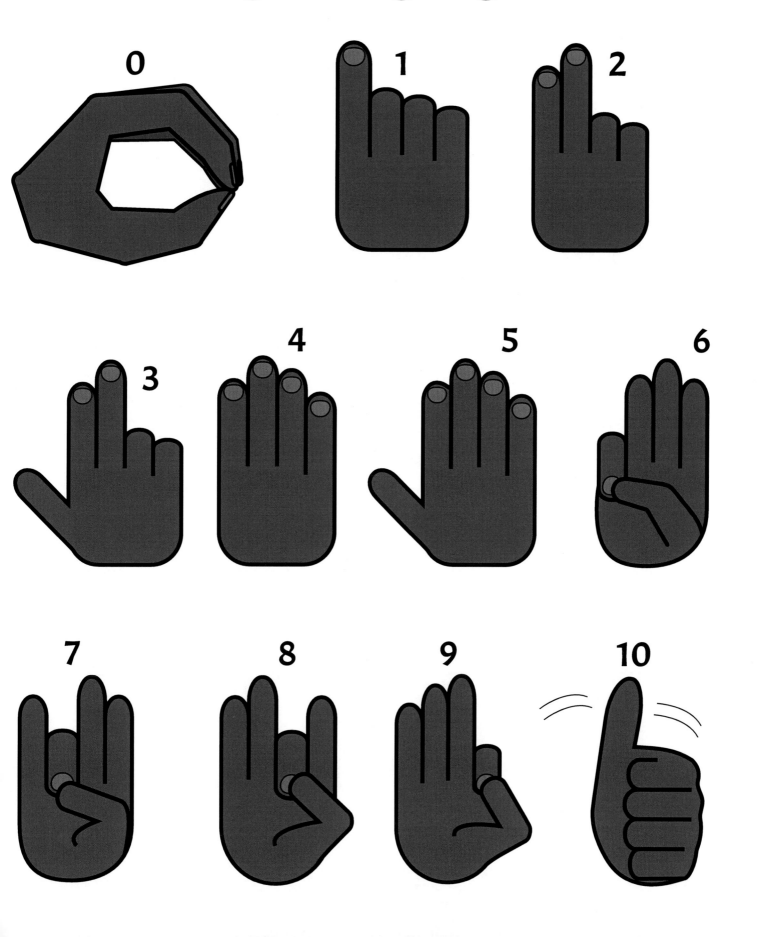

Numeral Angles

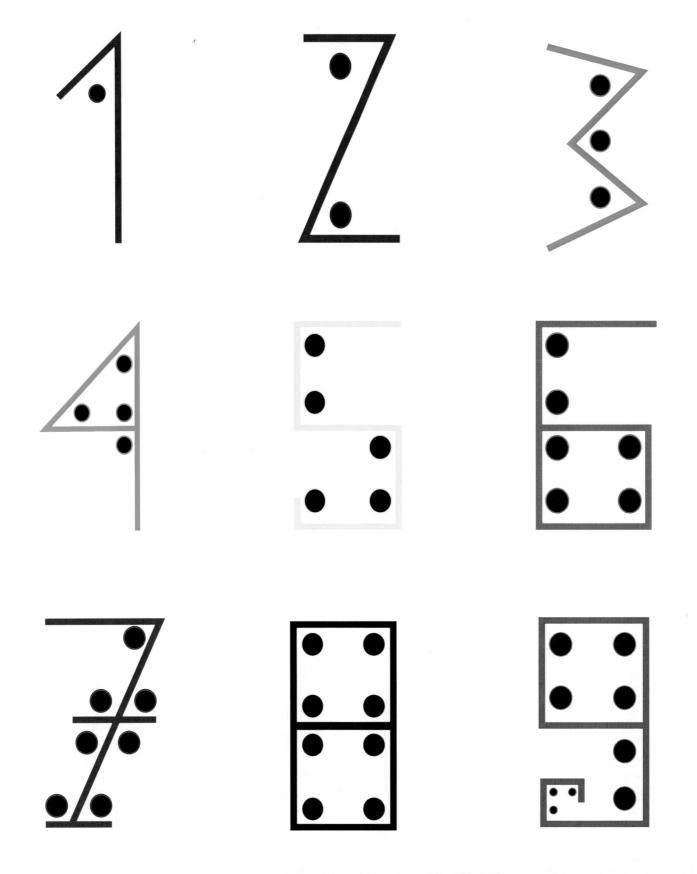

Equal Parts Angles

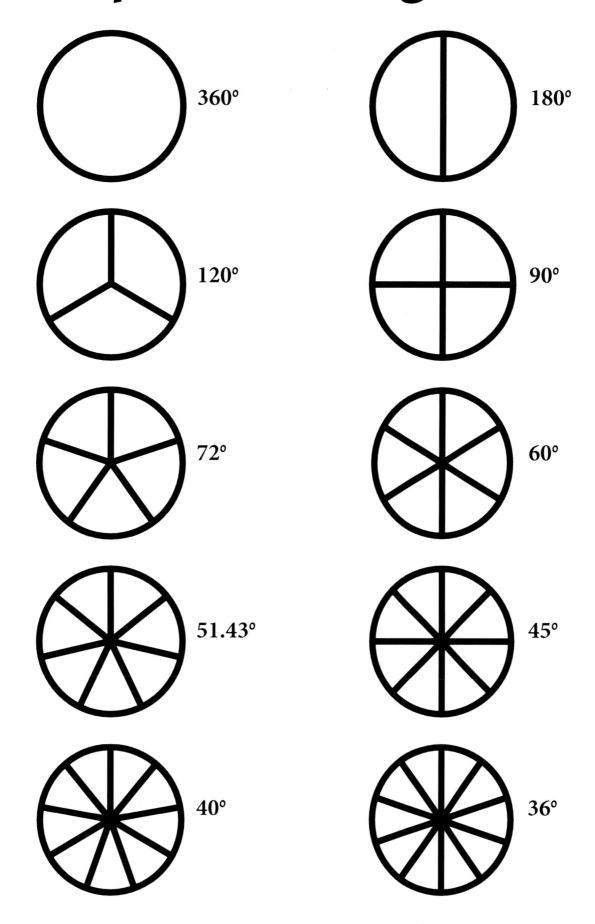

Made in United States
North Haven, CT
13 November 2021